GAUDÍ

Design Monographs

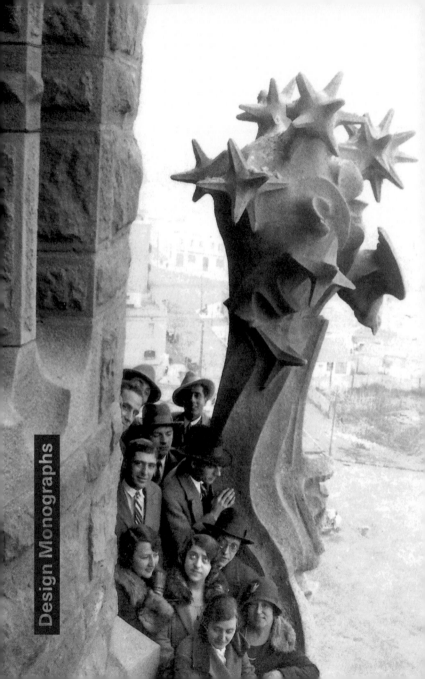

GAUDÍ

NAOMI STUNGO

Antoni Gaudí | Designer of residential spaces characterized by an inestimable *fin-de-siècle* "pleasure principle", and religious edifices of haunting solemnity and complexion. A man whose legendary life, works and even death were marked by extremes, Gaudí has been trumpeted as a genius and equally demonized by critics, writers and journalists.

Whether visionary or viper, Gaudí left behind an architectural legacy that continues to generate controversy, while his devotional, even iconic appeal within his native Catalonia has not noticeably decreased during the century since his bizarre death in Barcelona in 1926. On the contrary, in late 1998, the Cardinal of Barcelona nominated Gaudí for sainthood, proposing his beatification on the basis of a "profound and constant contemplation of the mysteries of the faith".

Both architectural and popular literature have contributed to Gaudí's apotheosis as the foremost patriarch of Catalan cultural heritage. Even within his own lifetime he was stereotyped as a mad architectural genius and has since, in essence, been mythologized either as saint or subversive. The very language of the Gaudí myth – that is, the myth's "text" – effectively embodies this polemic, revealing the extent to which we culturally link notions of fame, suffering and creativity in the portrayal of our artistic celebrities. Perceptions of Gaudí have been cloaked beneath a Janus-like garment of notoriety in our desire to understand his magical, fairytale buildings, which – rather like his life – conjure up impressions of sanity on one level, psychosis beneath; the sacred and the profane.

Gaudí's work was internationally highlighted during Barcelona's widespread urban renewal for the 1992 Olympic Games, and by the city's reception of the prestigious Royal Institute of British Architects' Gold Medal in March 1999. Despite the extensive renovation and redevelopment, however, one question of civic importance within Barcelona remains concerning Gaudí's magnum opus and "extraordinary stone vegetable patch", the Church of the Sagrada Família: "But what of the church?"

The Sacred

Referred to mockingly as a "pile of stones", the Expiatory Temple of the Holy Family begun in 1882 was entrusted to the thirty-one-year-old Gaudí as early as November 1883. Prior to this, Gaudí had completed no major independent architectural commission, although his first residential commission in Barcelona, the Casa Vicens (1878–85), was well underway. During 1882 he had worked alongside the medievalist Catalan architect Joan Martorell i Montells, under whose auspices he learnt an eclectic formulation of revivalist idioms in the popular neo-Gothic style. The younger architect's potential was clearly manifest, for it was with Martorell's endorsement in the following year that Gaudí obtained the esteemed post of director of works at the immense basilica of the Holy Family.

Gaudí's supervision of the architectural programme lasted forty-three years to 1926. Among the best-known anecdotes of Gaudí's life is that he resided in modest workshops in the church precinct during his final years: a decision no doubt dictated by a combination of logistical convenience, the effects of

Below. Gaudí showing the Sagrada Família to Cardinal Francesco Ragonesi in 1915.

increasing ill health and his fervent devotion to the realization of this monumental and enigmatic shrine. Such an apparently idiosyncratic gesture confirms the depths to which Gaudí had entrenched himself within a crafts ideology, if not an historicist allure of great past traditions of medieval cathedral building.

Born in Reus, Spain in 1852, Gaudí was trained as a craftsman in ornamental and utilitarian copperwork and metal smithing by his father. His natural orientation towards a very direct, hands-on approach to both the designing and making processes was well suited to his future architectural profession. It positioned him felicitously within the romantic and political ideologies of Catalonia's late nineteenth-century cultural resurgence movement, the *Renaixença*, of which both Barcelona and Gaudí were quickly at the heart.

Even within that cosmopolitan port and industrial city, the church precinct was itself conceived as the nucleus of a small "suburb" populated by sculpture and stone-cutting workshops, in addition to model-making studios. It even contained a parish school, which still survives, although it was moved to a new location in 2002 to allow for the church's expansion.

The complexity of the programme required a multiplicity of master craftsmen and engineers performing as a unified team committed to Gaudí's architectural agenda. Within their midst Gaudí himself is said to have scurried about attending to every manner of structural, engineering and aesthetic detail. The fulfilment of the undertaking, then, was not strictly weighted upon his shoulders – the notoriously fanatical, mad genius of art historical myth – but remained dependent upon established architectural tradition of expertise and multi-disciplinary endeavour.

All too often overlooked, this is well worth highlighting for despite the defiantly carcass-like embryo of the church that has presented its public face for so long, Gaudí bequeathed to Barcelona a legacy of co-operative workmanship to which generations of craftsmen like him have devoutly contributed. Historically, the church has been heralded not exclusively as Gaudí's endeavour, but in a more nationalistic vein as that of all Catalans, evoking John Ruskin's deeply romantic espousal of the authority of medieval

Opposite. The Sagrada Família under construction in the 1920s.

architectural practice with its intimate brotherhood of masons, cutters, pavers, tillers, glaziers and sculptors working in tandem with the local community, dedicated en masse to actualizing an architectural and devotional ideology intrinsically linked to the tangible, economic well-being of their "extended" community.

Gaudí's sympathies with the sociological dogma of John Ruskin's Arts and Crafts ideology, which he had studied, help to illuminate the allure of the crafts-orientated, communal ambience of the church precinct where he was able to focus his abilities ensconced within meagre studio quarters.

Gaudí saw the near completion of only one of three main façades of the church – that of the eastern Nativity; three of four eastern towers, less their kaleidoscopic, ceramic-encrusted pinnacles, then finished almost immediately following his death; the crypt begun in 1882 by the first architect, Francisco de Paula del Villar i Lozano, and completed to the latter's design; and a substantial segment of the outer apse wall. The building thereafter remained a masonry casing, more fantastic in its visual appeal by virtue of its motiveless and fragmentary state. As a church of atonement, resources for the new building were insufficient from the outset. Never receiving municipal assistance, it was to be constructed entirely from the private sector by donations, some of which Gaudí himself solicited on foot in Barcelona during the First World War.

Sons and grandsons of craftsmen who worked there with Gaudí continued a resolute familial association with the controversial but perpetually unfinished project. These have included Jordi Bonet, the Sagrada Família's chief architect from 1985 to 2012, an outspoken advocate of Barcelona's commitment to realizing Gaudí's plans. His advocacy was pitted against an opposition – formerly boasting as advocates, the so-called fathers of architectural modernism, Walter Gropius and Le Corbusier – which has consistently petitioned to suspend work on the church, arguing that additions in the aftermath of Gaudí's death are, at best, imitations or, at worst, kitsch.

Gaudí's church remains inflected towards the neo-Gothic idioms of his early career only in its emphatic height and ideological purpose. The building's first architect, Villar, was responsible for the conventional Latin cross plan and overall disposition. The building's imposing proportions are meant to harbour five naves, the central one measuring a formidable

Above left. Bishop's Palace, Astorga. **Above right.** Casa de los Botines.

95 metres (312 feet) in length, with the transept length two-thirds of that and 30 metres (100 feet) across. Its choir galleries could ideally accommodate a daunting 1,500 vocalists and perhaps seven pipe organs.

However, Gaudí inaugurated an increasingly dramatic rejection of any historicizing neo-Gothic approach, contradicting his own youthful influences and re-presenting with imagination the traditional typology for a basilican church.

Gaudí's training had essentially been an inculcation into neo-Gothicism. As an architectural student at Barcelona's Escuela Superior de Arquitectura, he became immersed in the popular stylistic approach of Barcelona's most persuasive medieval revivalist architects. He was subsequently exposed to the ethical medievalism of Joan Martorell and worked with Villar on a neo-Romanesque chapel at Montserrat Monastery. During this period Gaudí also assiduously read Eugène Viollet-le-Duc's neo-Gothic theories of structural rationalism in the recently published *Entretiens sur l'architecture*.

Nevertheless, his two early buildings considered the "most" neo-Gothic (see above) merely bow to medieval styling on their exteriors and in some external features. Both the Bishop's Palace, Astorga (commissioned 1887) and the commercial-cum-residential Casa de los Botines (1891–92) use neo-Gothic elements with sophisticated economy, such as tripartite glazing, corner turrets, pointed arches, French Gothic capitals and rounded towers. Motifs drawn from medieval secular precedents also appear and are combined by Gaudí in a thoroughly eclectic fashion. These buildings prove Gaudí's intimacy with medievalist styling and suggest the neo-Gothic typology that might have been used at the Sagrada Família, but wasn't.

His novel treatment of the eastern Nativity façade, surmounted by those looming parabolic bell towers, which measure approximately 100 metres (328 feet) each, is anything but conventional. For many years the most photographed section of the existing building, it provides the most tangible evidence of Gaudí's mature, increasingly aberrant architectural vision.

Gaudí's animated and interpenetrating surfaces confirm his interpretation of architecture as organic structure that expresses the growth potential and evolutionary properties of nature. As Rainer Zerbst has pointed out, "For Gaudí, however, nature consisted of forces that work beneath the surface, which was merely an expression of these inner forces. For example, he studied how stone blocks behaved when placed under pressure by putting them in a hydraulic press." The façade of the Sagrada Família is a purposeful visual statement of this architectural approach, and parallels the equally geological, but more tentative "jagged" undulations of his Casa Batlló (1904–06), and the broader, more intrepid triple façades of the famously "cliff-like" Casa Milà (1906–12).

On all three buildings Gaudí looked upon the rock-coloured faces as opportunities to meld sculptural plasticity with architectural mass; to the extent that it becomes impossible to see where one structural or decorative element ends and the next begins.

The enormous bell towers equally defy comparison with any architectural precedents outside of Gaudí's own oeuvre. Initially conceived as square, with Gaudí they evolved into rounded, majestic protuberances. Their tapering, futuristic appearance does not derive from antecedent Gothic spires, but rather from their idiosyncratic parabolic configurations, complemented by

Opposite. Nativity façade with bell towers, Sagrada Família.

The straight line belongs to men, the curved one to God.
Antoni Gaudí

an open network of square and columnar braces producing a honeycombed effect. Their aggressive upward thrust acutely expresses Gaudí's predilection for growth metaphors, the labyrinth of towers suggesting an otherworldly "forest in stone".

Similarly, figural sculpture depicting biblical scenes and meant to adorn the church throughout fulfilled not only a conventional didactic purpose, but also symbolic and metaphorical ones. Based by Gaudí upon a series of plaster moulds and photographs taken from living models, their implicit human fragility must be understood to be juxtaposed to the intrinsic, elemental brutality of the façade's pulsating surface.

The architect clearly intended the visual messages of the new church to be read in different ways and on a number of different levels as "cultural" language. In addition to architectural, symbolic and metaphorical imagery, he also adapted textual inscriptions to the fabric of the building. In so doing he identified the structure's entity as an adroit amalgamation of text and image; a result of the pairing of his somewhat raw creativity with his erudite and zealous religiosity.

The Sagrada Família is not so unlike most of Gaudí's other architectural projects in that it defies stylistic categorization. Nevertheless, it does have precedents within his own oeuvre that also show an exquisite interplay between surface, space and structure, setting the stage for the success of his daring innovations at the Sagrada Família.

The parabolic arch, one of Gaudí's most notorious personal trademarks, is worth focusing upon here, for although it appeared in both his secular and religious buildings, it is likely to have been developed not only for its structural efficiency, but to provoke an atmosphere of the sacred rather than the secular.

Opposite. Arches in the Casa Milà.

His experimentation with its potential may have begun as early as 1882; its first proper appearance was the stables of the Güell Pavilions (1883–87), where it facilitated the infusion of natural light through the arched openings in the roof.

At about the same time at the Palau Güell (1886–88) in Barcelona, Gaudí confidently manipulated the parabola as a significant engineering as well as theatrical feature in a residential setting of some magnificence. Here, the parabolic arch appears in two ways: firstly, in the twin arches of the entrance, and on bay windows above; secondly, as the main structural element creating the apparently monumental interior spaces grouped about the reception area covered by the substantial parabolic vaulting.

With the Colegio Teresiano in Barcelona (1888–90), Gaudí achieved a breathtaking degree of spatial and architectural abstraction in the internal hallways of this motherhouse of the Order of St Theresa of Avila. Here the parabolic arch is handled as the foremost architectural motif of the interior. The poetic temperament of its configuration and its ability to accommodate consecutively windowed curtain walls without the use of heavy, external buttressing use is exploited to create an atmosphere of meditative calm entirely appropriate to the setting.

Below. Arches in the Palau Güell.

The most dramatic precedents for the forceful treatment of the parabola at the Sagrada Família, however, are in some especially fantastic plans for two unexecuted projects, both known today through drawings.

Dating from 1892–93, the earliest of these sketches was for a church and monastery for the Franciscans of Tangier, and reveals the beginnings of Gaudí's ideas for the cluster of parabolic towers used subsequently at the Sagrada Família. Then in 1908, he sketched remarkably similar ideas for a hotel complex in New York City, again boasting groups of parabolic towers perhaps 200 to 300 metres (655 to 985 feet) in height. These towers are simply the silhouette of the parabolic arch twisted 360 degrees, resulting in "rotational parabolas" whose true symbolic meaning still remains unclear.

While working on the mature phases of the Sagrada Família, Gaudí was simultaneously engaged on another important commission for sacred structures: the unrealized chapel and incomplete crypt (1898–1917) of the Güell Colony in Santa Coloma de Cervelló. Gaudí's surviving drawings clearly suggest the church was envisaged as the fruition of the parabolic tower groupings imagined for the New York and Tangiers projects. Revealingly, or perhaps fortuitously, no project including this disconcerting feature was ever built and – although the towers are noticeably narrower – those of the Sagrada Família are not complete more than 100 years later. But for the small chapel planned for the Park Güell, this is only the second church of Gaudí's career.

The Güell Colony crypt, however, is extraordinary. Its slanting columns and arcuated structures disable conventional perceptions of interior space and architectural support. But for the exquisite craftsmanship of the brick- and basaltwork and the sophisticated arrangement of the many polychromed, ceramic surfaces, the crypt gives the impression of having been excavated from slanted fissures in the hillock of which it forms an organic part.

Within the crypt Gaudí excels in his gifts as a structural engineer. It is impossible not to enthusiastically praise such an enchanting and yet brutal spiritual space where the altar chapel ceiling suddenly proliferates in a cage of primitive arches and columns that seem to be driven by centrifugal force.

The unprecedented eccentricity of the structure is consistent with that of the Park Güell of about the same time. Both betray a symbiosis between architecture and nature that mark Gaudí's mature eclectic style and his increasingly confident subversion of established canons of form and function. His favouring of nature as the fundamental frame of reference for the invention of both symbolism and structure is extreme, while his expression of raw, unrefined power in form, texture, materials and space in concert divorces his work from superficial, populist expressions of Art Nouveau in both Barcelona and Northern Europe. What Gaudí does have in common with Art Nouveau practitioners is his harmonious synthesis of multiple materials and both crafts and architectural expression into a unique, unified whole in the manner of the *Gesamtkunstwerk* – the "total work of art". This approach, so evident in the Güell Colony crypt, is most apparent in his residential schemes.

The Secular

Gaudí was born a Catalan. During his formative years as an architectural student in Barcelona from 1869 to 1878, he witnessed the strengthening of the city's umbrella nationalist movement, which included both regionalists and separatists, and here developed the fervent Catalan sympathies that characterized his life and career. In Barcelona's architectural culture he was at the vanguard of the nationalist sentiment shared by the majority of leading Catalan architects including Francisco de Paula del Villar i Lozano, Martorell, Lluís Domènech i Montaner and Josep Puig i Cadafalch, whose largely regionalist ideology even infiltrated Gaudí's education at the Escuela Superior de Arquitectura where he matriculated in 1878. He belonged to study groups such as the Centre Excursionista, who journeyed to Catalonia's historic monuments, perceived as icons of the region's glorious past and whose study would inspire the assertion of national identity.

Two of Gaudí's earliest jobs carried further undertones of the ideology of the Catalan cultural resurgence movement known as the *Renaixença*. Joining Villar at work on a neo-Romanesque chapel at Montserrat in 1877, he worked briefly within an architectural style promoted among "national" idioms by *Renaixença* protagonists. In the following year he exhibited preparatory drawings in Paris for a new settlement comprising residential facilities and a factory for the co-operative of textile artisans at Mataro, a programme betraying *Renaixença* ideology in its paternalistic sentiment and the influence of John Ruskin's social ideology. By the time Gaudí began his first independent

Catalans have a natural sense of (the) three-dimensional that gives them an idea of things as a whole and of the relationship among things.
Antoni Gaudí

architectural commission, the Casa Vicens in Barcelona in 1883, he was saturated with a pietistic utopianism that professed cultural resurgence and argued for a unification of the ancient with the contemporary as the means to a better future.

In his secular commissions Gaudí willingly provoked issues of his Catalan identity. In his hands materials and motifs were used symbolically to invite reminiscences of Catalan culture.

The major secular monuments dating from his earliest period as an independent architect in the 1880s are qualified by their eclectic stylistic approach, but all show his ability to communicate political and social meaning through the visual vocabulary of architecture and decoration. Buildings such as the Casa Vicens, the rural villa El Capricho (the "caprice", "whim"; 1883–85) and the remarkably elegant Güell Pavilions with their latticework of honeycombed stucco are well known for their expression of a "Moorish", but more accurately *Mudèjar* style, at which Gaudí became an acknowledged master.

The *Mudèjar* style, an art and architecture of Islamic derivation arising on the Iberian Peninsula in the eleventh century, was revived during the late nineteenth century within a specifically Catalan context. It constituted a local re-elaboration of traditional forms, materials and techniques combining Christian with Arabic, Persian and North African elements in a hybrid style of decorative exuberance. It appeared in Gaudí's work and elsewhere as part

Above left. Tiles at El Capricho. **Above right.** Tiles at Casa Vicens.

of a synthetic, decorative approach at the vanguard of the Catalan medievalist revival, which also included the neo-Gothic idiom. *Mudèjar* motifs became signals particularly of cultural entrenchment and, as such, were translated into a highly graceful and sophisticated form of visual propaganda.

The exteriors of the Gaudí buildings named above are thoroughly indicative of his mannered interpretation of the *Mudèjar* style. The crowning minaret-like turrets recollect indigenous Islamic tradition, in their largely decorative rather than functional purpose becoming leitmotifs in Gaudí's oeuvre. The tower-minaret subsequently appears shamelessly upon his secular roof spaces, which increasingly become plateaux for expressive, sometimes even subversive architectural form, such as at the Palau Güell, and most dramatically later at the Casas Batlló and Milà.

A *Mudèjar* inflection is also seen in Gaudí's proclivity towards dense surface ornamentation and patterning, created by horizontal and stepped detailing of decorative brickwork and finely polychromed, ceramic cladding. At the Casa Vicens these features also make a very public statement about the patron who was an affluent brick and ceramic tile manufacturer, suggesting Gaudí's discriminating combination of design and craft was meant to help define, perhaps with political overtones, public perception of Barcelona's *haute bourgeoisie*.

An expressive and cosmopolitan use of polychromed ceramic tiling became one of Gaudí's stylistic trademarks, suggesting a personal penchant for crafts-based media. A consistently strong emphasis on materials in his work betrays his intrinsic understanding of craftsmanship and crafts-based methods as being at the very heart of good design. In this, he was a man of his time in Barcelona where a prominent crafts resurgence was fuelled by the desire to reassert past indigenous tradition.

Gaudí's Catalanist ideals were perhaps most in sympathy with those of his most important patron, the Catalan industrialist and paternalist, the Baron Eusebi Güell i Bacigalupi. He first met Güell in 1878 and would go on to design some of his most persuasive structures for this patron. Over twenty years, Güell commissioned from Gaudí a series of substantial projects, their authority and sheer creative drive attesting to the intimate and nurturing bond between architect and patron.

These included the Güell Pavilions outside of Barcelona, the Palau Güell, the crypt and church of the Colònia Güell, modest warehouses and a chapel at the Bodegas Güell, Garraf (1895–1901), and the chequerboard-like Park Güell (1900–14) overlooking Barcelona.

With Güell, Gaudí became ever more ensconced within Catalan cultural politics. At his patron's home he met with other avant-garde and romanticist artists, poets and novelists of the *Renaixença* movement, discussing among other topics the reformist writings of John Ruskin and the French neo-Gothicist Viollet-le-Duc, both of whom advocated a regionalist approach to architecture. Clearly Güell saw himself as a new patron of the emerging Catalan arts, while his prominent position in Barcelona's *haute bourgeoisie* allowed him to construct a pattern of patronage using contemporary design as a mechanism of federalist conservatism and bourgeoisie authority. Essentially, he employed Gaudí as part of an aesthetic power base which derived from the political and paternalistic affinities shared between the two. Gaudí upheld the primacy of the architect as "divine artificer" in the formulation and betterment of contemporary Catalonia, while Güell used Gaudí to position himself at the forefront of paternal benefaction, making tangible his own self-righteous feelings about the bearing of Barcelona's industrially based middle classes.

During the 1890s both Gaudí and Güell were closely aligned with the Cercle Artístic de Sant Lluc, a para-official, Catholic group of influence, composed of the artistic and educated who sought to renew urban society by means of an ideology based upon charity, artistry and morality. It boasted itself a guild of "Artisans of Beauty" referring to a pronounced crafts bias.

The Palau Güell is a palatial, grey marble-encrusted urban residence, also intended as a luxurious focus for *Renaixença* cultural activities. Its massive column between the entry portals of the ground storey exhibits the Catalan emblem. Built no doubt as a showcase for the forthcoming 1888 Barcelona World Exposition, the palace displays the patron's taste, aesthetic erudition and political persuasion. It also exemplifies Gaudí's synthetic incorporation of elements from *Mudèjar*, Gothic and Renaissance sources fused into a thoroughly individual statement.

The interior spaces are distributed about a magnificent central space rising through two storeys and supported by a parabolic vault lit from small, star-like punctures in the cupola. The central reception hall below, dedicated to drama, dance and musical performances as well as literary gatherings, is neither wide nor long, but overall feels enormous because of the vaulting, exhibiting Gaudí's tendency to exploit effects of Baroque illusionism.

The deceptively simple façade is punctuated by two archways containing an intricately woven wrought-iron lattice fabricated to include allusions to Gaudí's patron. Wrought-iron ornamentation was deeply indicative of Gaudí's aesthetic and allowed him to achieve an unlimited degree of self-expression via crafts-based skill. This is borne out early on in the delightful iron-work benches, arbours and little balconies of El Capricho, and thereafter throughout his oeuvre.

The grandiose and prison-like Dragon Gate linking the two small Güell Pavilions is, however, one of Gaudí's greatest realizations of exotic fantasy in wrought iron. Of ceremonial bearing, the gate gives access to a recreational estate. The dynamic tension of the design is equally two- and three-dimensional, relying on nervousness of line as much as texture. It displays a huge, terrifying dragon with splayed jaws and extended wings emerging from a twisted body. Defensive iron talons arise from the dragon's claw when the gate is opened – a less than subtle device of power and intimidation.

Gaudí's penultimate commission from Güell was for the chapel and crypt at the latter's model community with a factory, housing for industrial textile workers and a school at the Güell Colony, Santa Coloma de Cervelló. Although only the crypt was built, the concept betrayed Catholic reactionism against encroaching effects of secularization, as well as Güell's paternalist motives which, again, Gaudí was called upon to actualize.

A similar motivation inspired the Park Güell, a landscape of extravagance nestled in the hills above Barcelona. This extensive park was equally meant to express Güell's confidence in the reformist ideology of the *Renaixença*. It was conceived by Gaudí as a "garden suburb" accommodating as many as sixty individual middle-class households in a walled community, complete with infrastructure such as viaducts, avenues, play area, covered market and plaza. Only two houses were built, while the church planned to symbolically arise from the summit of the hill was never constructed. The site is significant for its ennobled synthesis of the sacred and the secular, the spirit and the senses, the structural and the ornamental. In effect, the Park Güell celebrated a middle-class "pleasure principle", underpinned by morality and family values but nevertheless manifest in Gaudí's unprecedented fusion of texture, colour, natural and artificial space and structural form.

Still popular as municipal grounds, the Park Güell is at once impish and surrealistic; a fairytale garden combining the ethos of Disneyland with that of an antediluvian Jurassic Park. The site is circumscribed by serpentine enclosing walls setting the festive tenor of the recreational area within, while barring "the other" from outside the perimeter. Sloping walled grottoes excavated from the hillside, and columns and walls constructed of rough-hewn rubble introduce the concept that nature itself generates architectural form. A visible alliance with nature in repeated motifs of animals, plants, rocks and caves is complemented by arbitrary mosaic patternings, which adorn the park's undulating structures. The polychromatic, tiled parapet-bench, which effortlessly curls around the flat roof of the market hall, is among the most famous examples of Gaudí's use of ceramic, porcelain and glass shards in abstract collages, which also embellish fountains and a family of enigmatic sculpted pets. There can be little doubt that with this commission Gaudí firmly established his reputation as an eccentric genius.

The Profane

Park Güell was the start of a critical period of Gaudí's mature work in which conventional architecture decomposes and he conscientiously begins to subvert accepted norms of structural form and space.

The Casas Batlló and Milà represent the clearest assertion of Gaudí's mature organic style and are the pinnacle of his achievement in design for secular buildings. The buildings arose near one another in the heart of Barcelona, each comprising multiple rather than single apartments. They constitute highly self-assured architectural statements, which were meant to be seen and meant to provoke.

The patrons of both buildings counted among Barcelona's industrial bourgeoisie for whom Gaudí redefined the very nature of an urban residence as a domestic utopia. In both instances the patrons clearly aspired to successfully compete within their milieu, making public declarations of architectural celebrity, therefore commissioning Eusebi Güell's architect. But for their origins in a regionalist, bourgeoisie ambience, both buildings would appear to be largely de-politicized, although the history of the Casa Milà was briefly touched by events of the *Semana Trágica*, the "Tragic Week", of July 1909.

During an episode of escalating anti-clericalism in Barcelona, the conservative Regionalist League, of which Gaudí and some of his patrons were members, provoked a violent repression of dissidents causing the deaths of eighty-three demonstrators and some anarchists to face execution. In the aftermath, sculptural representations of the Virgin and Child, along with religious dedications planned for the façade of the Casa Milà were rejected by the patron.

The unprecedented absence of straight lines and right angles either inside or without the Casas Batlló and Milà have caused them to be consistently described by reference to biology, botany, geology and zoology – a virtual plethora of scientific and pseudo-scientific terminology used to explain what Gaudí himself called their thoroughly "anti-classical" and "anti-historicist" character.

Gaudí's intentional evocation not merely of nature but more specifically of the emerging natural sciences is perhaps one of the most under-explored aspects of his architectural identity. During the late nineteenth century, religion and science were still simmering with animosity. But in northern Europe a handful of exceptional Art Nouveau precursors and early practitioners combined a keen pursuit of the natural sciences with parallel careers in design. Among these, for example, the works of Arthur Heygate Mackmurdo and Christopher Dresser, a respected doctor of botany, would have been accessible to Gaudí through British Arts and Crafts sources such as *The Studio* magazine. But it is not so much the point that their works embody osteomorphic linear swells and undulating organic surfaces as leitmotifs of the emerging Art Nouveau style, than that they acutely studied the natural sciences in and of themselves. In Mackmurdo's case, this also included the new social sciences as espoused in the evolutionary theory of, for example, Herbert Spencer.

Below. Casa Batlló.

Gaudí had unquestionably looked directly at artefacts of the natural sciences, perhaps at Barcelona's new science museum, or in populist but influential illustrated science publications, such as those of Ernst Haeckel.

His visual – not architectural – language in the Casas Batlló and Milà was drawn from palaeontological, as well as geological sources. At the Casa Batlló this is patently apparent in the fossil-like column of vertebrae, which appear to remain implanted within the rock-like stratum of the stairway. At the Casa Milà the cave-like articulation of windows and interior spaces betrays a similarly scientific tone, which in part then belies the steady claims that Gaudí's mature works, but for the excellence of their engineering, amount to nothing more than the musings of a madman.

Gaudí imitated such natural forms in order to create hybrid architectural statements, but because he rarely outright quoted the whole form of any organism, fossil or mineral aggregate, it would perhaps be unsound to suggest he studied materials of the natural sciences in minute detail. Furthermore, because he refuses to quote the whole, there is a feeling of things being only partial. This imparts to his work associations with the grotesque, fantastic and chimeric, especially in his recollections of marine organisms.

The sculptural tendencies in both buildings is equally pronounced, confirming Gaudí's complete transition to a conceiving of architecture

Here one can truthfully say that form does follow function – dripping, dissolving, re-forming, changing colour and texture; soft architecture, juicy architecture, the architecture of ecstasy. Robert Hughes, *The Shock of the New*

as lithe plastic form rather than immovable structure. Both buildings, but especially the Casa Milà, visually move of their own accord, pushing the tensile strength of materials to its very limit. By this time in his career, Gaudí had come to approach architecture – both religious and secular – as the incarnation of evolutionary theory, dependent upon laws of nature which dictate that all life, all structure, is in constant transition. Surely, he had found a means of reconciling religion with science; the sacred with the profane.

Legacy

Gaudí's death on 7 June 1926 abruptly ended his work on Sagrada Família at the pinnacle of his naturalistic style. As biographer Lluis Permanyer recounts, "Death came upon Gaudí suddenly. One afternoon he was walking, as was his custom, to the Church of San Felip Neri to pray, when he was run over by a tram ... because of his ragged appearance he was not recognized or given the emergency treatment he required."

It is Gaudí's preoccupation with the sacred that has dominated his legacy, as incarnated by the Sagrada Família. With its finger-like towers stretching above the Barcelona skyline, the project with which the architect remains most closely associated – and which for so long was known as the world's oldest construction site – now appears tantalizingly close to completion. Most of the structural work on the body of the church and its towers should be finished by 2026, a full century after his death, although additional decorative details will not be concluded until some time afterwards. For around a decade now, its form has been sufficiently complete for weekly services to be held within.

Despite this protracted gestation, significant architectural milestones have been passed at the church since the millennium. In 2002, construction began on the Glory façade to the south, one of three adorning the basilica. Representative of Christ's ascension to Heaven and his reign there, it will necessarily be the most imposing of the trio. More than twenty years later it remains incomplete, although the main access door to the church was fitted in 2009. The incorporation of text as an architectural element, seen in the decoration of the steeples, is carried through here too: its main door reproduces the Lord's Prayer in Catalan, with the Apostle's Creed set to appear elsewhere on the façade. (The main doors of the Passion façade are home to passages from the Passion of Jesus, in several languages.) All are reminders of the central theme of the church itself: the life of Jesus Christ.

The Nativity and Passion façades were completed in 1930 and 1976, respectively. They incorporate four bell towers apiece, making for one of the church's most distinctive features. (There will be twelve in total once the Glory façade is completed, each one dedicated to an apostle.) Gaudí lived to see only one of the Nativity's bell towers completed, that of St Barnabas. In 2005, UNESCO World Heritage Status was bestowed on the Nativity façade, along with the Sagrada Família's crypt and apse. Several of the architect's other remarkable buildings, including Casa Batlló and the Güell Colony's crypt, were also honoured.

The vaulting for the central nave was finished in 2000, and by 2010 – when construction on the church as a whole passed the halfway point – it had been covered and an organ had been fitted. In the same year, the building was formally declared a minor basilica by Pope Benedict XVI, who conducted a consecration mass on the site on 7 November, its proceedings followed by some 6,500 of the faithful within the church and an estimated 50,000 others without. Work also commenced on foundations for all of the church's naves, for the façades, vaults and columns for the central nave, apse, crossing and transepts. (Fears aroused by the construction of a high-speed rail network below the church's foundations remained groundless. It entered service in 2013.)

During the bulk of the church's construction history, stone was shaped on site, a skilled and time-consuming process. Yet Gaudí was fully aware that his basilica would be "an offspring of a long time, the longer the better", according to Buenaventura Conill i Montobbio, a close friend and architectural disciple. Gaudí was correct in ways that perhaps even he couldn't have foreseen, not least because some of his designs were geometrically so complicated that contemporary technologies struggled, and sometimes failed, to realize them. It took a later generation to fulfil such plans – another reason for the basilica's prolonged construction.

Jordi Faulí, chief architect at the Sagrada Família, in an interview with NHK, 2020, said: "[He devised] certain geometric shapes, that had never been used in architecture … and that allowed him to create these naturalistic forms that we see today … hyperboloids, paraboloids, double-twist columns … Moreover, this geometry, these structural themes that Gaudí suggested, are so clear that they have allowed us to follow the construction work according to his ideas."

A prime example is offered by the unorthodox and elegant double-twist helix columns that grace the central nave. Gaudí had tried out something similar at Park Güell, to create a sense of uplift, of linking Earth and Heaven. But for the basilica, he refined his approach, conceiving a column that combined historical precedents: the undecorated circular form familiar from Rome's Pantheon; fluted grooves; and Solomonic columns, which incorporate a rising helical twist. Effectively two overlapping Solomonic columns, twisting in opposite directions, the pillars taper gracefully towards the top, at which point the flutes that run along them combine. As each pillar rises, its cross-section changes from that of a polygon on the temple floor to a circle at the apex. Gaudí's insistence that structure should follow on from meaning is reflected in their conception: the polygons are star-shaped, thus these helicoidal columns symbolically link the terrestrial with the celestial.

But although Gaudí had mapped out the 3D mathematical models for these innovatory columns, the challenges of actually realizing them had frustrated earlier architects. It took decades for technology to catch up with his visionary schemes. In 1979, Mark Burry – later to become an executive architect at the basilica – began incorporating CAD (computer-aided design) systems into the construction process, going on to produce a computer-generated study of the building. CAM (computer-aided manufacturing) technology provided a complementary asset, producing components that were computer-generated. (Both had been utilized in the automotive and aerospace industries since the 1960s to mathematically describe shapes, broadening the possibilities for design.)

In July 1988, the Sagrada Família purchased a CNC (Computer Numerical Control) milling machine to produce stone sections and, in November 1989, the first piece of stonework to be produced using these technologies was machined – for the Column of Lleida, which was eventually completed in January 1991. Going forward, the degree of precision made possible by such methods would also save on time, money and wastage. (Today, 3D printing is also utilized to create plaster models.) Computer-generated design and manufacture has led to off-site working becoming increasingly more common, though this became an inevitability as the structure of the basilica filled out, reducing the space available for the timber and masonry yards and design office. Jordi Faulí also commented that "the computers made it possible to analyze Gaudí's original project properly and to draw it precisely according to Gaudí's geometries. And also to give accurate information to the builders."

More or less simultaneously, Frank Gehry was employing CATIA (computer-aided three-dimensional interactive application) technology to design the landmark fish sculpture hovering over a retail court within Barcelona's 1992 Olympic Village. As at the Sagrada Família, the software would prove of inestimable value in helping Gehry's office to execute ambitious and unorthodox building projects, not least the Guggenheim Museum Bilbao.

More than fifty different types of stone have been used in the building to date, but one of the challenges brought about by its lengthy gestation has been the exhaustion of some of the quarries that provide them. Moreover, some of the original stonework is so old that it has had to be refurbished. The initial source of sandstone for the basilica was Montjuïc, the hill that overlooks Barcelona, whose quarries supplied material for the bell towers adorning the Passion and Nativity façades, as well as many of the city's other buildings. They provided a siliceous stone notable for its range of colouration and strong consistency, but by 1957 supplies were dwindling and quarries were shut down. A refashioning of Barcelona's Olympic Stadium in 1988 provided a further 1,000 cubic metres (35,315 cubic feet) of the stone, with more stone recycled from old buildings that were demolished in subsequent years. Alternatives have also been sourced from abroad, recently including the Brinscall Quarry near Chorley in Lancashire.

Other stones required for the church include blue granite from Brazil, the colour of which makes it symbolically appropriate for use on the tower of the Virgin Mary, and Blanco Cristal granite from Madrid, its pure whiteness and strength making it ideal for the core of the Jesus Christ tower. Iranian red porphyry, figuratively apt to represent Christ's blood and structurally strong enough to be used for the four central columns at the centre of the cross vault within the basilica, support the central dome dedicated to Jesus Christ.

Controversy has dogged the project almost since its inception, and continues to do so. Many locals complain that the area is being degraded by the millions of tourists (around 60,000 per day before the Covid-19 pandemic struck) that descend annually on the site. The mooted construction of a huge staircase leading to the main entrance, which will necessitate the demolition of some local housing blocks and the forced relocation of families and local businesses, has also prompted outrage.

In February 2010, the Sagrada Família was awarded the Barcelona City Award in Architecture and Urban Planning, for its ongoing efforts to realize Gaudí's ambitious plans. The move infuriated both high-profile architects and ordinary citizens, however. They felt aggrieved that the jury had not chosen a contemporary, forward-thinking project – not least because Barcelona was in desperate need of innovative housing – and suspected that the decision was based partly on a desire to stimulate tourism.

There was debate too about the appointment of Josep Maria Subirachs, one of the sculptors (along with Jaume Busquets and Etsuro Sotoo) chosen to decorate the church's façades. Subirachs had accepted the commission in 1986 on condition that he be allowed to live within the precinct in a small flat, as Gaudí had, and that he should be permitted to work to his own designs, rather than follow the master's lead. His creation of 100 block-like, angular stone figures for the Passion façade aroused particular outrage in some quarters – not least because they were so different in appearance from the figuration on the opposite Nativity façade, which were more in keeping with the lithe plasticity characteristic of Gaudí's style. Despite this, they (along with

I will grow old but others will come after me. What must always be conserved is the spirit of the work, but its life has to depend on the generations it is handed down to and with whom it lives.
Antoni Gaudí

He managed to build nature using architecture.
Jordi Faulí, 2020

his doors for the Glory façade, a sculpture of St George and a half-bust of Gaudí) were declared a Cultural Asset of National Interest by the Catalonian government in 2019. Gaudí the architect might have found them a distraction from his original vision, but might equally have applauded Subirachs as an artist from a later time whose contribution adds its own stamp to his master plan.

By 2015, chief architect Jordi Faulí – the ninth incumbent of that role since Villar – was able to announce that 70 per cent of the building had been completed (at the time of Gaudí's death, barely a quarter had been finished). He also revealed the next stage: the erection of six towers, which began the following year. Four of these were dedicated to the Evangelists, with a higher fifth for the Virgin Mary. The tallest of all (at 170 metres/558 feet) will be dedicated to Jesus Christ, and on its completion the Sagrada Família will become the world's tallest church.

It would be another four years before the first stone panels for these towers arrived on site. Features all but invisible to those on the pavement below – including twelve wrought-iron pointed stars, and exquisite blue-and-white trencadís mosaic – were added to a shaft atop the tower of the Virgin Mary. (A bishop who once asked Gaudí why he bothered with details that no one could see received the reply, "Your Grace, the angels will see them.") The tower was finally completed in 2021, when it was crowned with a twelve-point steel-and-textured-glass star of Bethlehem; on 8 December that year, the star was illuminated and the Archbishop of Barcelona, Juan José Omella, performed a mass and blessing of the tower.

Irrespective of when the finishing touch is applied, the Sagrada Família already represents an outstanding achievement for the ages, a testament not only of faith but also to the skill and dedication of the myriad crafts-men, engineers and architects who have served it down the decades.

Opposite. The nave, Sagrada Família.

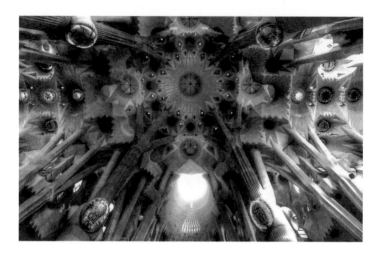

Above. The Sagrada Família basilica.

A masterpiece of structural engineering, it remains true to Gaudí's central maxim of taking inspiration from the natural world and its architect – God.

Look upwards from the central nave to the complex web of vaulting above, supported by arrestingly tall columns (the tallest a full 45 metres/148 feet high) of various hues, all sloping inwards, and which sprout stone branches at their apex. For these, Gaudí took as a model the load-bearing properties of eucalyptus tree. Along with the parabolic curves of the interior, the columns help to share and transfer horizontal weight. This reduces the load on the walls, eliminating the need for bulky external flying buttresses (as in his earlier Colegio Teresiano), resulting in a more graceful overall shape to the basilica and allowing for more, and larger, windows. With light filtering down through circular apertures in the vaulting, and inwards as a rainbow of warm hues from the stained-glass windows on the walls, the effect is similar to standing in woodland as sunlight breaks through the foliage. Such was Gaudí's intention.

Flora and fauna bedeck the exterior of the basilica, as with so many of Gaudí's iconic works elsewhere in the city, along with biblical narratives. Each of its walls differs from the others stylistically. The overall impression is of an organic force growing upwards, its steeples straining towards heaven.

Complex rounded geometrical shapes such as parabolas, helicoids and hyperboloids aren't there simply for aesthetic appeal: they help refine the basilica's acoustics and the quality and abundance of light within it. (Light is closely identified with faith within the Christian religion, making its presence of theological as well as practical importance.)

In calculating the optimum design for the basilica's windows, façades, vaults and columns, he used his own ingenious "hanging chain" models to create a mirror-image scale replica of the building. To do so, he suspended connected bags of lead – precisely measured to mimic the relative weight of the vaults and roofs – from strings. The latter were pulled taut by the bags, and their incline provided Gaudí with the exact dimensions of the arcs that he would need.

The famously protracted construction process has been hobbled by a number of unique factors, not least Gaudí's death, which scuppered progress for around a decade. The works have twice been forced to shut down altogether. In July 1936, as the Spanish Civil War broke out, a group of young anarchists targeted the Sagrada Família, which to them symbolized nationalism and the Catholic clergy that, by and large, sided with it. They set the crypt ablaze and destroyed many plaster models and plans in Gaudí's workshop, necessitating a painstaking and time-consuming reconstruction of his original intentions.

In March 2020, construction ground to a halt again owing to the Covid-19 pandemic, which prompted an unwanted hiatus lasting several months. And in 2018, having established that – astonishingly – no official permit for the construction had ever been issued by the local council, the city's authorities issued the Construction Board of the Sagrada Família with a fine of around €35 million, to be paid over 10 years.

Then again, Gaudí understood that such an immense and ambitious undertaking would take a commensurately long time to come to fruition. He would have known that the construction of Barcelona's Cathedral of the Holy Cross and Saint Eulalia lasted from the thirteenth to the fifteenth century, while Rome's St Peter's Basilica was 120 years in the making. And as "God's Architect" once dryly observed, his client was in no hurry.

Overleaf. Mosaic, Park Güell.

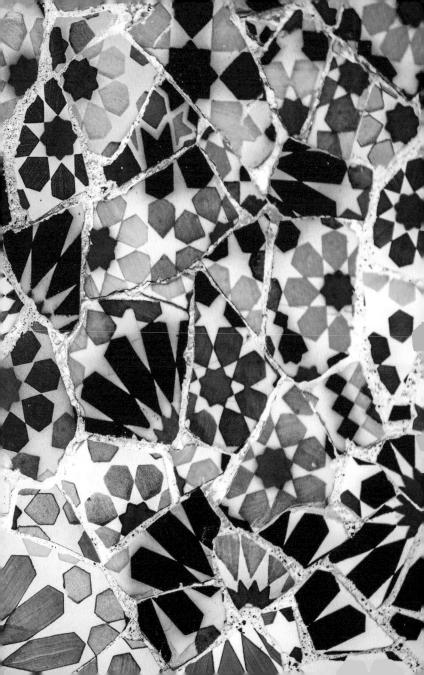

[01, 02, 03] El Capricho, 1885.

[04, 05] Dragon Gate, Güell Pavilions, 1887; [06, 07, 08] Casa Vicens, 1885.

[09] Colegio Teresiano, 1890; [10, 11, 12] Palau Güell, 1888.

[**13, 14, 15**] Bishop's Palace, 1913.

[16, 17, 18] Casa Batlló, 1906.

[19, 20, 21, 22, 23, 24] Casa Milà, 1912.

[25]

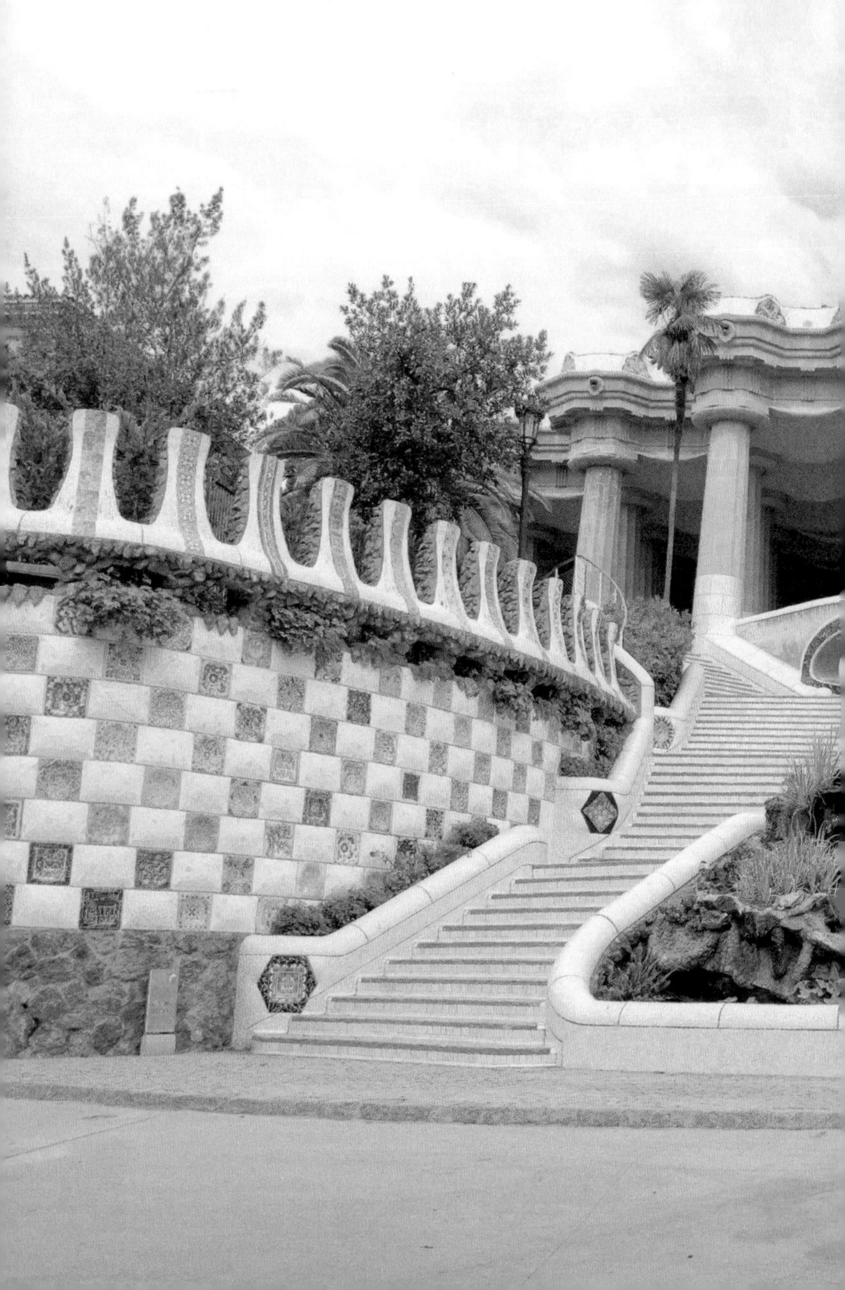

[25, 26, 27, 28, 29, 30, 31, 32, 33] Park Güell, 1914.

[34, 35, 36] Güell Colony Crypt, 1917.

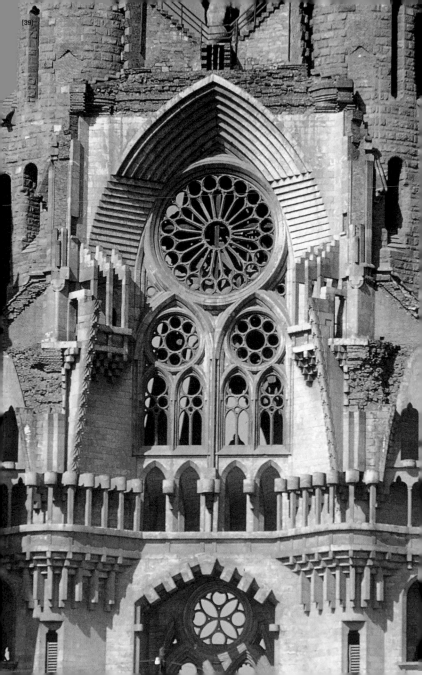

[37, 38, 39, 40, 41] The Sagrada Família, ongoing.

44

RESPONGUE ANEU A LA C
CASA D'TAL I DIGUEU LI EL MESTRE DIU LA
VA MEVA HORA ÉS A PROP A CASA
SOPAR PASQUAL AMB ELS MEUS DEIXE
A CASA TEVA ELS DEIXEBLES VAN COMPLI
EL QUE **JESÚS** ELS HAVIA ORDENAT I
PREPARAREN EL SOPAR PASQUAL
ARRIBAT EL CAPVESPRE JESÚS ES POSÀ
A TAULA AMB ELS DOTZE MENTRE SO
PAVEN DIGUÉ US HO ASSEGURO UN
DE VOSALTRES EM TRAIRÀ MOLT EN
TRISTITS LI ANAVEN PREGUNTANT
UN RERE L'ALTRE ¿NO SÓC PAS JO
SENYOR? JESÚS RESPONGUÉ UN QUE
SUCA AMB MI AL MATEIX PLAT ES QUI
EM TRAIRÀ EL FILL DE L'HOME SE'N VA
TAL COM L'ESCRIPTURA HA DIT D'ELL
PERÒ AI D'AQUELL QUE EL TRAEIX I MÉS LI VAL
DRIA NO HAVER NASCUT JUDES EL QUI
EL TRAIA LI PREGUNTA ¿NO SÓC PAS
JO RABÍ? ELL LI RESPONGUÉ TU HO HAS DIT
MENTRE SOPAVEN JESÚS PRENGUÉ
EL PA DIGUÉ LA BENEDICCIÓ
EL PARTÍ I TOT DONANT LO ALS DEIXEBLES
DIGUÉ PRENEU MENGEU NE AIXÒ ÉS EL MEU
COS DESPRÉS PRENGUÉ UNA COPA
DIGUÉ L'ACCIÓ DE GRÀCIES I ELS LA DONÀ
TOT DIENT BEVEU NE TOTS QUE AIXÒ ÉS LA
MEVA SANG LA SANG DE L'ALIANÇA VESSADA
PER TOTHOM EN REMISSIÓ DELS PECATS
US ASSEGURO QUE DES D'ARA JA NO BEURÉ
D'AQUEST FRUIT DE LA VINYA FINS AL
DIA QUE BEURÉ AMB VOSALTRES
EN EL REGNE DEL MEU PARE DESPRÉS
CANTAREN ELS SALMS VAN SORTIR CAP
A MUNTANYA DE LES OLIVERES

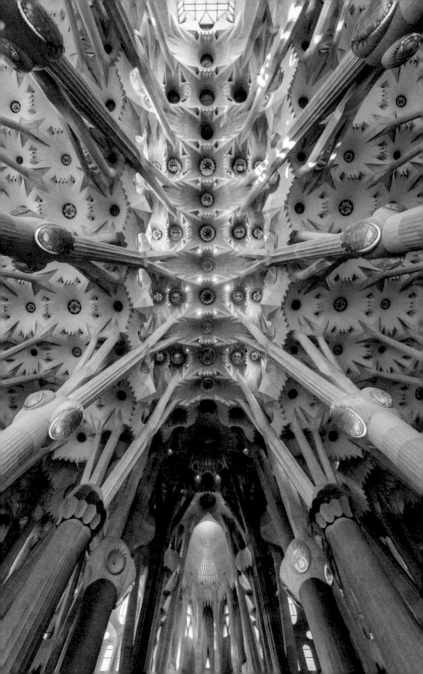

45

[42, 43, 44, 45, 46, 47] The Sagrada Família, ongoing.

Picture Credits

The publishers would like to thank the following sources for their kind permission to reproduce the pictures in this book.

Alamy /Album 8, 49/Arcaid 2 (people at the Expiatory Church in the 1920s), 48/Bildarchiv Monheim 11r /GL Archive 7/Ivan Vdovin 11l /Julian Money-Kyrle 13. **Arcaid** /John Edward Linden 94. **Corbis** /Adam Woolfitt 50, 51, 74b, 106/Alamany & E. Vicens 58bl, 58br/Charles and Josette Lenars 44t, 58tl, 58tr, 75t, 76/ Charles E. Rotkin 96/Hans Georg Roth 54–5/K. M. Westermann 61/ Mark Garanger 74t/ Martin Jones 66/Michael S. Yamashita 75b/Patrick Ward 77–81, 97, 99/ Peter Aprahamian 44b/Ramon Manent 15, 59, 89. **Eye Ubiqitous** /Linda Miles 95. **Kea Publishing** 46tl, 46tr. **Shutterstock** /4kclips 62–3/BearFotos 16/catwalker 72–3/basiczto 92–3/DFLC Prints 90–1/Diabluses 38/EQRoy 40–1/Guillem Verges 98/Ikonya 56/Isa Fernandez 42–3/Ivan Marc 104/Jaroslav Moravcik 65, 67, 68–9/Juan Enrique del Barrio 57/Pajor Pawel 3–4 /Pen_85 20r/Radu Bercan 102/saiko3p 39/silverfox999 52, 53/Sweetland Studio 88/Tao Qi 47/wolffpower 20l. **Unsplash** /Ana Bórquez 82/Andrea G 45, 46br/Ashwin Vaswani 64/David Salamanca 103/ Dimitry B 84–5/Florencia Dalla Lasta 60/Ian Kelsall 107/Jenny Marvin 105/ Kristijan Arsov 86–7/La Partida Eterna 34/Maria Krasnova70–1/Mahdi Samadzad 100–1/Martijn Vonk 83/Mihály Köles/Nick Fewings 33/Pedro de Sousa 46bl/Raimond Klavins 35, 36–7/Tomáš Nožina 108.

Every effort has been made to acknowledge correctly and contact the source/copyright holder of the images. Welbeck Publishing Group apologizes for any unintentional errors or omissions which will be corrected in future editions of this book.

Opposite. The stained-glass windows of the Sagrada Família.

First published in 1999.

This revised and updated edition published in 2023 by OH! Life
An imprint of Welbeck Non-Fiction Limited, part of Welbeck Publishing Group.
Based in London and Sydney.
www.welbeckpublishing.com

Text and Design © Welbeck Non-Fiction Limited 1999, 2023
Cover image: Detail of Casa Batlló. Courtesy of Hercules Milas/Alamy Stock Photo.

A CIP catalogue record for this book is available from the British Library.

ISBN 978-1-83861-116-3

Associate publisher: Lisa Dyer
Contributing writer: Rob Dimery
Design: www.gradedesign.com
Production controller: Felicity Awdry

Printed and bound in China

10 9 8 7 6 5 4 3 2 1